People
Eat with their *Eyes*

How to Create an Effective Book Trailer

La'Tanyha Boyd

People Eat with their Eyes: How to Create an Effective Book Trailer
By Lá Tanyha Boyd

This book was printed in the United States of America.

Connect with Lá Tanyha Online!

www.latboyd.com

TABLE OF CONTENTS

INTRODUCTION

People Eat with Their Eyes. A book trailer (video) captivates people and draws them in. Having a Video Book Trailer for your book will provide you with opportunities to connect with your audience and sell more books!

Book trailers are a great marketing tool and is quickly gaining popularity among publishers and successful authors to help promote books and encourage people to read them. Bestsellers have them – why not you? Introduce your book and get potential readers excited!

From Wikipedia, the free encyclopedia:
A **book trailer** is a <u>video</u> advertisement for a <u>book</u> which employs techniques similar to those of <u>movie trailers</u> to promote books and encourage readers.[1] These trailers can also be referred to as "video-podcasts", with higher quality trailers being called "cinematic book trailers".[2] They are circulated on television and online in most

common digital video formats.[3] Common formats of book trailers include actors performing scenes from the book akin to a movie trailer, full production trailers, flash videos, animation or simple still photos set to music with text conveying the story.[4] This differs from author readings and interviews, which consist of video footage of the author narrating a portion of their writing or being interviewed.[5] Early book trailers consisted mostly of still images of the book, with some videos incorporating actors

Online book trailers can be effective tools for marketing and gaining potential readers. With that said book marketing efforts need to be *productive* not just *active*.

Your book trailer allows potential readers to see the essence of your novel or non-fiction book in an entertaining short film. The aim of an effective book trailer would say YES to the following questions:

- Did it grab your attention?
- Do you want to share it with someone?
- Do you want to watch it again?
- Where you moved (touched with emotions)?
- Most importantly, are you going to check out the book now?

Online book trailers can be an effective tool for book marketing as well as creating book buzz for an upcoming release. With more and more video production tools becoming accessible and easy to use, you might think about using an online book trailer to promote your book. Here's how to get started laying out your book trailer.

Your book trailer can have a compelling effect; when well produced and marketed. A book trailer is a video advertisement for a book which employs techniques similar to those of a movie trailer. Just like an effective movie trailer, you want too, convey that same essence for your book without giving too much away.

Book trailers are a great marketing tool and is quickly gaining popularity among publishers and successful authors to help promote books and encourage people to read them. Bestsellers have them – why not you? Introduce your book and get potential readers excited!

THE ANATOMY OF A BOOKTRAILER

Technical ways to create a video.

There are free services like Moviemaker, ScreenFlow and also Animoto.com for animations.

Do your research and gather info, brainstorm for ideas

Watching other book trailers will provide you with insight about how to effectively present a preview of a book when making your own trailer. Think about the types of previews for movies you have seen. Have you ever watched a movie trailer that went on for way too long? By the time it's over, it seems as though you've seen all the key moments in the film.

Look at book trailers for books similar to yours Check out the competition — what book trailers are out there that look similar to yours? What kind of page views are they getting? You can look at hundreds of sample book trailers on sites like YouTube and Vimeo. Go to individual book publisher's sites for their authors' book trailers.

The purpose of your trailer
Of course, you want eyeballs on the video, but think about your book's potential and how best you think they will be engaged by your video. Do you want to inform? Entertain? Educate? Be sure to outline your book trailer goals and ideas.

Select only Vital Elements
Most book trailers don't need to be much longer than a minute or two. This may seem like a daunting task at first, especially if the book was filled with intricate storylines, complex characterization and interwoven themes. However, keep in mind that the purpose of a book trailer is simply to capture the attention of the viewer and get them interested in reading the book. Begin by thinking about a few

intriguing elements of the book and how you can bring them together into a video.

Highlight the Main Characters

Introduce a few compelling characters at most and leave the minor characters out. Focusing solely on these key characters will help in allowing you to leave out many aspects of the story that are nonessential. Also, book trailers do not need have to show exactly how the characters look. Precise appearances are often left out intentionally because it leaves the reader free to visualize the characters and imagine more on their own.

Stick to Major Plot Points

Stick to shorter statements rather than those that are too wordy when writing a script in order to draw people in to the story. Overloading the trailer with unnecessary details about the plot and settings is not necessary. Give a broad overview of what the book is about in a concise manner. Highlight what makes the story unique or interesting while not giving away the unexpected twists and turns that take place. One useful approach is to mix in memorable or thought-provoking quotes from the book. Many book trailers will end by posing a question or with a suspenseful cliffhanger finish. Such techniques leave the viewer wondering about an uncertain outcome and what direction the story will take.

Let Pictures Tell the Story

You can get images from iStockphoto.com and also creative commons from Flickr.com. You can get video from lots of different sites including archive.org.

Making a storyboard before gathering images is helpful in planning out the entire sequence of images from beginning to end. Estimate how long each image will appear, perhaps about five seconds or more on average, in order to calculate the approximate total time of the video. The amount of time each image appears can vary and depends on what type of pacing you want to set. Remember that even though you are describing a book, you are using a visual medium. Other elements such as the text and music can be arranged to fit within the flow of the video.

A captivate book cover, author photo, still photos from the book—all of these key elements are essential in developing/producing an eye catching book trailer.

Another key element in production if your budget allows would be to have strong video team. Production takes time and money and people with skills. Think about who you know with video production and/or editing skills? Try to get them on board or at least get advice. Do you need to hire someone? Actors? Videographers? What's your budget? Will your publisher help defray costs?

Set the Tone

The mood or emotion expressed in the video will often be a reflection of the genre and basic premise of the book. Some of the factors that influence the tone of a book trailer and can add some feeling to it include the pacing and the music. These aspects influence whether the video is somber, upbeat, frightening, dramatic, etc., and allow the video to build in intensity.

Choose Music

Remember to ensure your music choice is royalty-free. Proper use of music and sound can make or break your video or film production. For music, make sure it is upbeat and appropriate for your book and also the audience. Remember to be aware of copyright. You need to use royalty free music and images.

Incompetech is one of my go-to places for great royalty free music. The site was created by composer Kevin MacLeod and has tons of music, categorized by genre and feel. In the site's FAQ you'll see that the music on the site is free to use for your video soundtrack. Kevin just asks that you place a credit within the video.

FreeSoundtrackMusic.com provides exactly what it advertises – royalty-free tracks for use in films, YouTube videos, games or other multimedia productions. Some of the music on the site does cost money. However, a lot of it is labeled as "FREE" and can be easily downloaded and added to your video production.

Partners In Rhyme has got all sorts of great stuff, from free music loops to sound effects, midi files and more. Some of the royalty free music on Partners In Rhyme costs money, but they've got a selection of free music loops and full-length tracks for free download as well.

Beatpick offers a great selection of licensed music and if you are using it in a non-commercial or non-profit production it's free. Once you've chosen a song that you want to use, click on "License Song" and choose "Non Commercial projects."

BOOKTRAILER DESIGN OPTIONS

The sky is the limit when it comes to producing your trailer. Many people use text, pictures, animation, voiceovers, and real people to make the trailer to look more like a movie trailer. Here are four examples of trailers you can draw inspiration from.

Book Trailer Example #1: Using Text

Simple Text can be effective. Below is a book trailer I produced using Animoto.com for pre-order(s) of my Bestselling book Spiritual Food for Thought: 31 Inspirational Quotes to Jump Start Your Day!

http://animoto.com/play/OaqcnmRsmbZ 2qkv0Bmpl1g

If you notice the scripting was simple but yet effective with only music and type:

- Book Cover
- Type book title
- Tag line
- Timeline New Release-Author name
- Call to Action
- Website
- Closing with book cover

Music was used as a back drop

Book Trailer Example #2: Using Animation, Text, & Music with Vocals

While text is effective, you may be interested in adding a little flair with animation, text, and music with vocals.

Written and produced by Bestselling Author Alphina By Faith Of Woman Renewed: A 21-Day Journey To Changing any Story and Becoming the Virtuous New You!

http://youtu.be/nVrhtwu6_GM

This book trailer was produced using Animoto

Book Trailer Example #3: Using Hand Drawn Pictures, Animation, Music with Vocals, Headshot of Author

Written and produced by 2013 Mrs. Essence LaQuisha Hall Author of Positively Bodyful!

http://animoto.com/play/iUleUhoxlT8Kd
StkNZ0xrQ

Features: Within the pages of this book were hand drawn characters of which were used in the book trailer.

Book Trailer Example #4:
Using Real People and Voice Over

This book trailer was produced by Bestselling Author Tamika Hall Meet Me At the Altar.

This was done using an IPhone to record the footage, iMovie to edit the footage together. And Audacity (free audio software) to edit audio

http://youtu.be/fJp4aq57mlE

IMovie (usually comes free with a MAC computer.)
Movie Gallery usually comes free with a windows platform computer

Trailer elements:

- Voice-Over

- Text
- Music
- Live Actors

Be sure to include basic book information in your book trailer

It's easy to get caught up in the creative processes of writing and producing a dynamic book trailer—so it's important that you include the basic information that helps ensure that potential book buyers can find your book when they want to.

Don't forget to include:

❖ *Prominent mentions of the book title*
Depending on the length of your trailer, ideally, you should mention the book's title at least three times in the book trailer dialogue or voice over, as well as have it appear in text at least twice during the course of the trailer, most importantly at the beginning and the end.

❖ *Call to action to motivate potential book buyers*

"Call to action" are advertising parlance for making it known to the consumer exactly what you want them to do. The end of your book trailer should have a call to action. Some examples of typical calls to action are: "Get more information at www.latboyd.com."

"Buy a copy of My Great Book at Barnes & Noble, Amazon.com, and your favorite independent bookseller—or wherever books are sold."

Social media contact information

❖ Book trailers should prominently display the book or author website and any and all social media addresses— Facebook , Twitter, Pinterest, etc. Make sure that you display this information for the length of time it takes for someone to be able to thoroughly read it, slowly. The most natural place for this information to appear is at the end of the book trailer, before the credits. It can even appear with the call to action.

Credits for the folks who helped you with the trailer

❖ Online video conventions—like film or television—suggest that you list credits for those people who helped work on your book trailer. Especially if you received any video or online production services for free or at a reduced cost, it's good book karma—as well as customary—to give credit where credit is due.

Distributing Your Video

Go Viral by using other video platforms
Video platforms like YouTube and Vimeo have created a great conduit for book promotion via online video book trailers. Like commercials—only (usually) cheaper to produce and all-but free to distribute, the right book trailer can help spread the word about your book to a wide audience.

The ideal, of course, would be for a book trailer is to "go viral," and reach hundreds of thousands—or millions—of viewers. A more realistic (and perhaps even more practical) goal is to create a book trailer that gets passed along from potential reader to potential reader—like minded people who are truly interested in the book's subject matter and might actually buy the book, rather than just appreciate your video production   skills.

Top Leading Video Platforms:

About Animoto

For your video designs, consider using Animoto.com. It's FREE and you can upgrade as your budget allows. Very easy to use, lots of options to choose from. Check them out. http://animoto.com/

In the works since 2005, Animoto was founded with the vision of inspiring people to share their lives through the magic and power of video. Animoto's founders include veterans of the entertainment industry and have produced shows for MTV, Comedy Central, & ABC, studied music in London, and played in indie rock bands in Seattle.

Today, Animoto is a video creation service (online and mobile) that makes it easy and fun for anyone to create and share extraordinary videos using their own pictures, video clips, words and music.

Simply upload your pictures and video clips, choose your style, add words and music, and click the "produce video" button. Then, Animoto's cinematic technology does its magic and in minutes brings it all to life with a beautifully orchestrated production you can share with family and friends.

Millions of people actively use Animoto for everything from special occasions like birthdays, weddings and trips, to sending a quick special greeting, or just to share everyday moments.

Based in New York City with an office in San Francisco, The entire Animoto team is a passionate and innovative group devoted to helping more people experience the power of video for sharing their lives.

About Vimeo

Vimeo® is the high-quality video platform for creators and their audiences. Vimeo's mission is to empower and inspire people around the world to create, share and discover videos. Vimeo has 20M registered members and reaches a global monthly audience of more than 100M. Founded in 2004 and based in New York City, Vimeo, LLC is an operating business of IAC (NASDAQ: IACI). https://vimeo.com/

Video Editor Similar to iMovie but for PC?

Nowadays, Apple's Mac and Microsoft's Windows is the main operating systems for personal users. Many people use both Mac and Windows PC computers - usually Windows at office, while Mac at home. Someone may also have transferred from Mac to Windows for its more and more optimized features. If you're previously a Mac user and familiar with iMovie, now want to edit videos on your Windows PC computer, you need an iMovie for PC video editing software. http://www.imoviepc.com/

iMovie for PC Alternative
- Import video from computer or capture from camera
- Enhance video with useful video editing

tools
- Add special effects and good-looking transitions
- Export to PC, burn to DVD or upload to YouTube

Movie Maker

Whether you prefer Hollywood or the indie scene, you're the director with Movie Maker.

Import and edit slide shows and videos

Quickly add photos and footage from your PC or camera into Movie Maker. Then fine tune your movie just the way you want it. You can move things around, speed it up or slow it down—it's up to you.

Edit the soundtrack and add a theme

Enhance your movie with audio and a theme. Movie Maker adds transitions and effects automatically so your movie looks polished and professional.

Share your movie online

Once your movie is ready, share it online on Facebook, YouTube or other social networking and video sharing sites. Send a link to your movie in an email to family and friends so they won't miss it.

Fiverr.com

Fiverr is a global online marketplace offering tasks and services, referred to as 'gigs' beginning at a cost of $5 per job performed, from which it gets its name. The site is primarily used by freelancers who use**Fiverr** to offer a variety of different services, and by customers to buy those services. http://www.fiverr.com/

- Video & Animation
- Music & Audio

About the Author

Lá Tanyha Boyd, is a Bestselling Author of Spiritual Food For Thought: 31 Inspirational Quotes to Jump Start Your Day! Lá Tanyha has traveled around the world as an Empowerment Coach, Transformation Strategist, and Inspirational Speaker delivering messages to jumpstart your day and vision, all the while infused with Faith, Hope, & Determination leaving you with a mindset of I CAN DO THIS! Challenging others to Take Action to go higher in their careers, fulfill their goals and walk in their purpose.

Hosting a global radio broadcast of Spiritual Food for Thought Global Radio has afforded her the honor of empowering others across the globe to follow their dreams and to live life with purpose, passion, fire and determination.

Life is all about living and when we can have Spiritual Food, it nourishes us like nothing else.

Answering the call to minister, Missionary Là Tanyha has been working in the vineyard for over ten years, and is a Licensed Missionary.

Là Tanyha is a mentor and a powerful Inspirational Speaker, facilitator with a heart and fire for God and His people.

Là Tanyha has helped dozens of authors in establishing their brand and online presences. With over 20 years of marketing and as the founder of FAB Virtual Tours

Là Tanyha has assisted Indie & National Best Selling Authors with the promotion and marketing for newly release fiction and non-fiction, poetry and inspirational along with books of affirmations.

Note From the Author: Reviews are gold to authors! If you've enjoyed this book, would you consider rating it and reviewing it on Amazon's La Tanyha Boyd Page:http://www.amazon.com/gp/entity/-/B00EWPGPT4/ref=cm_sw_su_e

Faith ABeliever~FAB Virtual Tours

P.T. Barnum once said... "Without publicity a terrible thing happens...NOTHING!"

Gaining visibility is essential for any entrepreneur or author. One of the best ways to gain visibility today is via the internet, and a virtual tour. Social Media plays an important role towards the success of virtual tours AND also after the virtual tour is over.

Virtual Book Tours is one of the best ways to get your book noticed by potentially thousands of new readers! FAB Virtual Tours staff will walk you through the process of embarking on a virtual tour for your book, business, music, and or ministry. Providing, simple but yet effective strategies for getting your product and your message in front of thousands.

Sign up for a free FAB Virtual Book Tour consultation: bit.ly/RTL5rH

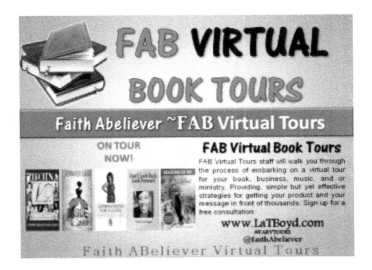

Have you written a book, recorded a CD, or started that business and you're asking yourself, "What Happens Now?" Well this is the time to let the world know that you exist. FAB's Marketing/Publicity/Coaching team is available to bring you out of obscurity and to the masses. Not only will your presence be elevated, but you will be mentored and taught to continue to do the work yourself.

Connect with FAB today to be empowered and inspired to market and leverage our ministry and brand. www.latboyd.com

Spiritual Food For Thought Global Radio:
Tune in:
http://www.blogtalkradio.com/faith-abeliever

Are You Ready To WALK in Your GREATNESS? #JSYD Jump Start Your Day! *Book Empowerment Coach Lá Tanyha Boyd, for your next event:* Most Requested Topics: Self-Empowerment of Lighten the load of 'Stinkin-Thinking;' & Build You're Career 'Change Your Seat.'

To Book a Speaking Engagement: www.latboyd.com

PEOPLE EAT WITH THEIR EYES

LA' TANYHA BOYD

www.ingramcontent.com/pod-product-compliance
Lightning Source LLC
Chambersburg PA
CBHW060933050326
40689CB00013B/3070